HUMBLE & KIND

HUMBLE
&KIND

TIM McGRAW

INTRODUCTION

I t is a rare moment when a song comes along that speaks equally to the world and to the individual. A song that transcends. A song that reaches into the heart of everyone who hears it. *Humble and Kind* is one of those songs. I feel blessed to have been chosen to be the conduit to deliver its message in this day and time.

The wisdom of this song came to me at the right time in my life and, I believe, at a great time of need for civility in the world. When I first heard it, it took me back to all the advice I heard growing up and, more importantly, it made me reflect upon the people who gave it to me. I thought about my grandfather. I thought about my mother. I thought about my high school coach and many friends along the way. These are the people who shaped my view and helped to set me along my path in life by their words and their actions. I was raised to be polite to everyone, no matter what side of town they lived on or color of their skin. I was encouraged to be generous with people who had less. I learned that I was responsible to my family and my community. As an adult, I can't help but think about these people and be grateful for what they taught me. Even if I don't always make the mark, I know where it is.

When I undertook the recording of the song, it was a time of transition for all of us in our home. We were faced with the reality of a daughter going off to college to face a new chapter of her life. As a family, we would be living without her. As parents, we had that moment to pause and reflect—is she ready to be on her own? Did we tell her everything she needs to know? I think every parent thinks, "Did I tell my kids this enough? Did we do this part right?"

The lyrics speak to me in a universal sense, too. They speak to that moment when you look in the mirror and ask yourself, "Am I doing the best I can do to be kind and humble?" We all fall short, but are we focused on the right things? Cultivating humility and exercising kindness are actions that form the very backbone of respect and compassion. Maybe they are simple in form—just to say "please" or "thanks." These little acts shape our global attitude for how we treat each other. How you act in the small things is how you act in the big things.

Part of the power of art is that it can enkindle each person to reflect and act—this song certainly accomplished that. At the end of the day, especially in these times, it's important to be reminded how impactful it can be simply to be kind to others; to show respect, compassion, and tolerance; to support diversity; and to have the strength to be humble in the midst of it all.

Humble and kind. I think kindness is the more straightforward of the two. We all see such meanness in the world today, but the way to counter it is with kindness—and not just to speak about kindness, but to be kind. Kindness comes in so many shapes and sizes. From the smallest act in helping someone with an inconvenience to a grand act such as donating an organ to someone in need: kindness. And there is a fulfillment that is realized in being kind. There is a beautiful diversity to kindness.

Humility, on the other hand, is something that you work on. It's a tightrope walk, a balancing act of the very emotions that propel achievement: proud, but not boastful; good, but not self-righteous; confident, but not arrogant; grateful, but never entitled. Sometimes we only truly learn humility when we lose our balance and fall off to one direction or the other—but it's important to keep trying. Humility is acting from a core belief that we are all equally worthy. It requires us to lend a hand to the next guy, because that next guy *is* us. Humility believes that our humanity defines us, not our achievements.

There's a lot negative in the world, but there's a lot of beauty in the world, too. There are a lot of people who are really trying to do the right thing for the right reasons. I think that any time you can highlight the good, any time you can bring it to the forefront and acknowledge it, that's a good thing. That's what music does in a lot of ways. Music reminds us of our higher calling. It encapsulates parts of our lives, brings to mind (in an instant) something from the past, but also inspires us in the present moment. I hope *Humble & Kind* does for you what it does for me: provoke me to reflect upon my values, instill them in my children, and share them with the world.

—Tim McGraw

You know there's a light
that glows by the front door
Don't forget the keys
under the mat

When childhood stars shine

ALWAYS
STAY
HUMBLE
&
KIND

Go to church 'cause
your mama says to
Visit grandpa every
chance that you can
It won't be wasted time
Always stay humble and kind

Hold the door,
say please,
say thank you

Don't steal,
don't cheat,
and don't lie

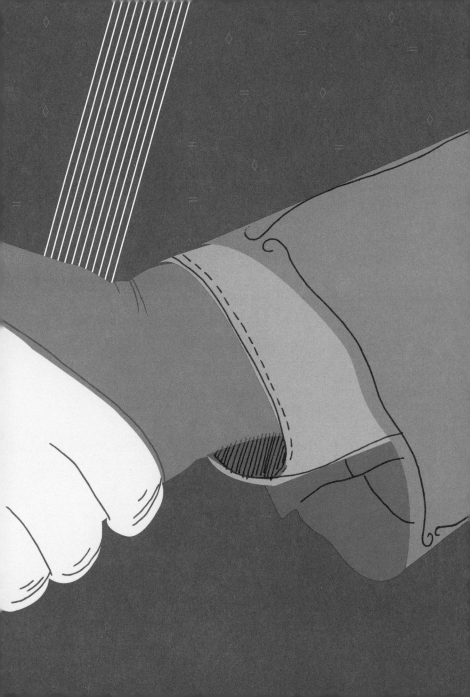

I know you got
mountains to climb
but

When the dreams you're
dreamin' come to you
When the work
you put in is realized
Let yourself feel the pride but
Always stay humble and kind

Don't expect a free ride
from no one
Don't hold a grudge
or a chip and here's why
Bitterness keeps you
from flying

ALWAYS STAY

HUMBLE & KIND

PATIENT

LO
VE

KIND

Know the difference
between sleeping
with someone
And sleeping with
someone you love
"I love you" ain't no
pickup line, so
Always stay humble and kind

Hold the door,
say please,
say thank you

Don't steal,
don't cheat,
and don't lie

I know you got mountains
to climb but
Always stay humble and kind

And when the dreams
you're dreamin' come to you
When the work you
put in is realized
Let yourself feel the pride but
Always stay humble and kind

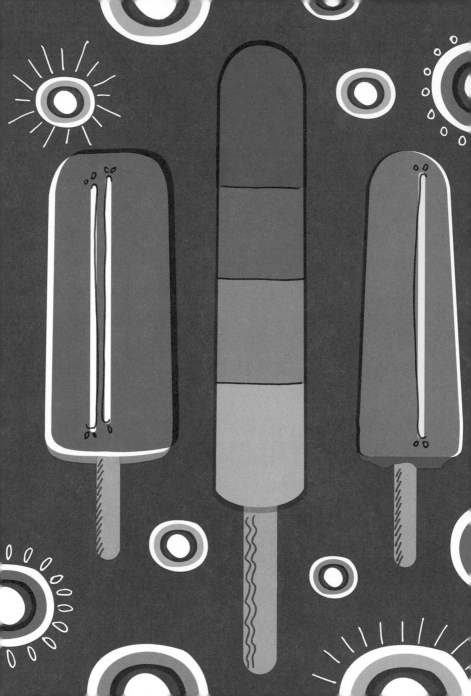

When it's hot,
eat a root beer Popsicle
Shut off the AC and
roll the windows down
And let that summer
sun shine

Don't take for granted
the love this life gives you

When you get
where you're going,
don't forget,
turn back around
Then help the
next one in line

ALWAYS STAY HUMBLE & KIND

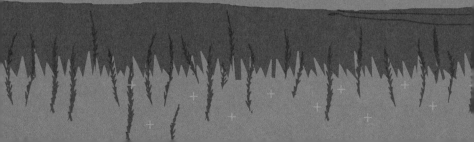

EPILOGUE

Often on school days when the house is quiet, I sit at my dining room table with my guitar in my lap and stare out the front window. Usually I mess with the guitar and see if a melody will pop out of it.

I was thinking of my kids (as parents often do) and taking a mental inventory of the lessons my husband and I have tried to teach them. We have five children, at the time ages 10–25, each born with a different compass, a different set of sails, and a different anchor. I decided to write a list: a list of things I want them to know, a list of things I sometimes forget and want to remember. The basics. The simple rules that our grandparents told us and our parents reminded us of and we all want for one another. It's only because I'm a songwriter that the list rhymed and came out in a three-chord progression. I always say that songs are just love letters we keep in our throats. Imagine you wrote your kids a letter and Tim McGraw sang it back to them.

It's not the songwriter's job to interpret each line—that's the listener's work. But I believe we are genetically wired to be kind. There will be blessings and there will be challenges—that's just how it is. But if every emotion stems from love or fear, maybe every action can stem from humility and kindness. And doesn't being nice make us all feel better?

Music has always given me more than I have given it. This song is melodic truth of that. The reaction I have received to this simple little song has been nothing short of overwhelming. Every time someone thanks me for writing it, I want to thank them for listening to it, Tim for sharing it, and my kids for inspiring it.

—Lori McKenna

ABOUT THE AUTHOR

Tim McGraw has sold more than 40 million records worldwide and dominated the charts with thirty-six #1 singles. He's won 3 Grammy Awards, 16 Academy of Country Music Awards, 14 Country Music Association Awards, 10 American Music Awards, 3 People's Choice Awards, and numerous other honors. His iconic career achievements include being named the BDS Radio's Most Played Artist of the Decade for all music genres and having the Most Played Song of the Decade for all music genres with "Something Like That." He is the most played country artist since his debut in 1992, with two singles spending over 10 weeks at #1 ("Live Like You Were Dying" and "Over and Over"). His critically acclaimed acting skills were highlighted in the award-winning movies *Friday Night Lights* and *The Blind Side*. Connect with Tim at: TimMcGraw.com, Facebook.com/TimMcGraw, on Instagram @TheTimMcGraw, on Twitter @TheTimMcGraw, and on Youtube at youtube.com/TimMcGraw

NEIGHBOR'S KEEPER ADVISED FUND
OF THE COMMUNITY FOUNDATION OF
MIDDLE TENNESSEE

Founded by Tim McGraw and Faith Hill in 2004 out of their desire to help people in need and encourage the spirit of neighbors helping neighbors, Neighbor's Keeper seeks to strengthen communities by contributing to diverse projects with primary emphasis on children's initiatives.